Things to Know About Convertible Debt

Disclaimer:

The information contained in this book is provided for general informational purposes only. While every effort has been made to ensure that the information is accurate and up-to-date, The Author makes no representations or warranties of any kind, express or implied, about the completeness, accuracy, reliability, suitability, or availability with respect to the information, products, services, or related graphics contained in the book for any purpose.

The Author disclaims any liability for any loss or damage, including without limitation, indirect or consequential loss or damage, or any loss or damage whatsoever arising from loss of data or profits arising out of, or in connection with, the use of this book.

Readers are solely responsible for determining the appropriateness of the information contained in this book for their specific purposes and should seek professional advice before acting upon any information contained herein. The Author shall not be liable for any damages of any kind arising from the use of this book or the information contained herein.

Table of Contents

Introduction

Convertible debt is a financing tool that has gained popularity among startups and investors in recent years. This type of debt allows investors to convert their investments into equity at a later stage, usually during a funding round. The process can be complex, and it requires a good understanding of the terms and conditions involved.

In this book, you will find a complete glossary of terms related to convertible debt, from basic concepts like "debenture" and "coupon" to more intricate terms such as "anti-dilution provision" and "multiple liquidation preferences." Whether you're a startup founder, an investor, or simply interested in the world of finance, this book will serve as a valuable resource to help you navigate the world of convertible debt. With clear explanations and examples, you'll be able to grasp the ins and outs of this financing tool and make informed decisions that align with your goals.

10

Forced conversion

Accredited Investor

A type of investor who meets certain qualifications such as high net worth or income, and is allowed to participate in certain investment opportunities, including convertible debt offerings.

Accruals

Refers to the accumulation of interest on a convertible debt that is not yet paid. Instead of receiving cash payments, the interest is added to the principal amount of the debt. This increases the total amount owed to the creditor and affects the conversion rate of the debt.

Active Conversion

This occurs when a convertible debt holder chooses to convert their debt into equity prior to the maturity date. The conversion may be triggered by certain events or based on the debt holder's decision.

Adjustable Conversion Price

This is the price at which convertible debt can be converted into equity. An adjustable conversion price allows for the price to be adjusted based on certain factors, such as additional funding rounds, to ensure that the debt stays relevant and maintains its value.

Adverse Selection

This refers to the risk that only risky companies will choose to issue convertible debt, leading to a higher likelihood of default or failure. Adverse selection can affect the interest rate charged on the debt as well as the terms of the convertible debt agreement.

Affordability Test

This is a test used to determine whether a company can afford to issue convertible debt based on its current financial position. The affordability test may take into account factors such as cash flow, earnings, and other liabilities.

Aggregate Principal Amount

This is the total amount of convertible debt issued by a company. The aggregate principal amount can be used to determine the total amount of equity the debt can be converted into.

Amortization

The process of paying off debt over time through regular payments that include both interest and principal, leading to a gradual decrease in the outstanding balance. Convertible debt instruments can have different amortization schedules depending on the terms.

Angel Investor

A private individual who provides financial backing to early-stage companies, often in the form of equity or convertible debt, and may also offer guidance and expertise. Angel investors can help startups raise capital through convertible debt offerings.

Anti-Dilution Protection

A provision in a convertible debt agreement that can protect investors from the dilution of their ownership stake in the event that the company issues new shares at a lower price per share than what the investor initially paid.

Any and All Offering

This refers to an offering of securities in which the company offers to purchase any and all outstanding convertible debt at a specified price. This can be beneficial for both the debt holders and the company, as it simplifies the conversion process and allows for a more streamlined capital structure.

Appraisal

The process of determining the value of an asset, property, or business using various criteria and methods. In the context of convertible debt, companies may conduct a formal appraisal to set a conversion price for the debt, which would allow investors to convert into equity at a set valuation.

Arbitration

This refers to the resolution of disputes between parties through the use of an arbitrator or third party. Some convertible debt agreements may include an arbitration clause, which can be used instead of going through the court system to settle any disputes that may arise.

Asset-Backed Convertible Debt

This refers to convertible debt that is secured by specific assets owned by the company. This can provide additional security for the debt holder and increase the likelihood of repayment.

Asset-Based Lending

A type of lending that is backed by collateral, such as equipment, inventory, or real estate. Some convertible debt agreements may require the company to pledge assets as collateral to secure the debt.

Assignment of Rights

This refers to the transfer of rights from one party to another. Convertible debt agreements may include provisions for the assignment of rights, such as the right to convert debt into equity or the right to receive interest payments.

At-Market Offering

This refers to the selling of securities at the current market price. Convertible debt can be offered through an at-market offering, allowing for more flexibility in the conversion process and potentially attracting more investors.

Automatic Conversion

This occurs when a convertible debt automatically converts to equity upon the occurrence of a specific event, such as an initial public offering (IPO) or a certain amount of funding being raised. This can be beneficial for both the company and the debt holder by simplifying the conversion process.

Bondholder

An investor who holds a bond, which is a debt security that pays periodic interest and has a maturity date. Convertible bonds are a type of security that can be converted into equity at a certain price or on a certain date.

Bridge Financing

A short-term financing solution that is intended to provide temporary funding until a longer-term financing option becomes available, such as an equity round. Convertible debt can be a popular form of bridge financing because it can provide startups with access to quick capital without the need to immediately set a valuation.

Buyback Clause

A provision in a convertible debt agreement that allows the company to buy back the debt at a certain price or on a certain date, usually with a premium. This can provide an incentive for investors to agree to the terms of the convertible debt offering.

Call Option

A contractual right that allows the issuer of securities, such as convertible debt, to redeem those securities prior to their maturity date. Companies may include a call option in their convertible debt agreements as a way to manage their debt balances and take advantage of changing market conditions.

Conversion Discount

The conversion discount is the percentage off the market price of the equity that the investor pays for the right to convert the convertible debt into equity. It provides the investor with the potential for increased returns upon conversion.

Conversion Event

The conversion event is the trigger that allows the investor to convert the convertible note into equity. It's typically tied to the company's financial performance or milestones.

Conversion Premium

The conversion premium is the percentage above the conversion price that the investor pays for the right to convert the debt into equity. It provides the investor with the potential for increased returns upon conversion.

Conversion Price

The conversion price is the price at which the convertible debt can be converted into equity. It's fixed at the time of the issuance of the convertible note and determines the conversion ratio.

Conversion Ratio

The conversion ratio is the number of shares of common stock that the investor will receive upon conversion. It's determined by dividing the principal amount of the convertible note by the conversion price.

Coupon Rate

The coupon rate is the interest rate that the company pays on the convertible debt. It's fixed and paid out periodically until maturity. The coupon rate is used to calculate the minimum return on the investment.

Debenture

A term in convertible debt that refers to a type of unsecured bond that is not backed by collateral, such as property or assets. Convertible bonds may be issued as debentures, which means that they do not have any specific collateral backing them up.

Debt Financing

The use of debt instruments such as convertible debt to raise funds for a company. Convertible debt allows companies to raise funds without diluting existing equity shareholders.

Debt maturity

A term in convertible debt that refers to the date when the debt becomes due and payable. Convertible bonds may have a fixed maturity date or may be perpetual.

Debt-for-Nature Swap

A type of convertible debt where a company agrees to invest in environmentally friendly projects as a way of paying off their debt. The conversion of the debt into equity shares is contingent on the company meeting certain environmental criteria.

Debtor-in-Possession Financing

A type of convertible debt used by companies that have filed for bankruptcy to fund their operations during the restructuring process. The conversion of the debt into equity shares may be used as part of the company's restructuring plan.

Debt-to-equity ratio

A term in convertible debt that measures the amount of debt used to finance a company compared to the amount of equity. The higher the debt-to-equity ratio, the greater the financial leverage of the company.

Default risk

A term in convertible debt that refers to the likelihood that a company will default on its debt obligations. Convertible debt may be considered to have lower default risk than other types of debt because the option to convert the debt into equity provides some protection to the investors.

Defeasance

A provision in convertible debt that allows the issuer to "defeat" or extinguish the debt by purchasing securities that are sufficient to cover the principal and interest of the debt.

Derivatives

Financial instruments that derive their value from an underlying asset, such as convertible debt that derives its value from the underlying equity shares it can be converted into.

Derivatives market

A term in convertible debt that refers to the market where derivative securities are traded. Convertible bonds may be traded in the derivatives market along with other types of derivative securities.

Dilution

A term in convertible debt that refers to the reduction in the value of the existing shares. When a company issues convertible debt, it automatically dilutes the ownership of existing shareholders. This means that the ownership percentages of existing shareholders will decrease as more shares are issued.

Dilution Protection

A provision in convertible debt that protects existing shareholders from excessive dilution. Dilution protection can come in the form of anti-dilution clauses or a cap on the number of equity shares that can be issued upon conversion.

Dilutive conversion

A term in convertible debt that refers to the conversion of the debt into equity, which results in dilution of the existing shareholders. Dilutive conversion may occur if the conversion price of the debt is lower than the market price of the stock.

Discount

A term in convertible debt that refers to the difference in value between the conversion price of the debt and the market price of the stock at the time of issuance. A convertible bond may be issued at a discount to its face value, which offers investors an opportunity to own equity in the company at a reduced cost.

Discount Rate

The interest rate used to calculate the present value of future cash flows from the convertible debt. The discount rate takes into account the market interest rate, credit risk, and the time frame of the debt instrument.

Discretionary Convertible

A type of convertible debt where the issuer has the discretion to choose whether or not to convert the debt into equity shares. This type of convertible debt tends to have lower interest rates than traditional debt due to the added benefit of the conversion option.

Dividend yield

A term in convertible debt that refers to the income generated by a security. In a convertible bond, the dividend yield is usually lower than in a regular bond because investors have the option to convert the bond into equity.

Dollar-Cost Averaging

A technique in which an investor purchases a fixed amount of convertible debt at regular intervals, reducing the impact of fluctuations in the market.

Early Conversion

Early conversion is an option for the convertible debt holder to convert the debt into equity before the maturity date arrives. Some convertible debt agreements may require prior company approval or fulfillment of certain conditions before early conversion.

Effective Interest Rate

The effective interest rate is the interest rate that is paid on the convertible debt, which takes into account the value of the option to convert the debt into equity. The premium paid for this option to convert generates a lower effective interest rate than the stated interest rate.

Embedded Conversion Option

An embedded conversion option is a derivative security within a convertible bond that acts as a call option, giving the holder the right to convert the bond into a predetermined number of shares of the issuing company. This option value is built into the pricing of the convertible bond and is usually the primary motivator for investors to purchase it.

Equity Clawback

An equity clawback provision is a feature of some convertible debt offerings that requires the issuer to repurchase a portion of the converted shares from the holder if a specified event occurs, such as a takeover or bankruptcy. This provision protects the interests of the existing shareholders by reducing potential dilution in such situations.

Equity Conversion Ratio

The equity conversion ratio refers to the number of shares you'll receive for each dollar of debt that you convert. This ratio is set by the company issuing the convertible debt, and it can vary based on several factors, such as the current stock price, the conversion price, and the terms of the debt.

Equity Floor

The equity floor is a provision in a convertible debt offering that sets the minimum number of shares that would be issued to the debt holder in the event of conversion. This floor limits the dilution of existing shareholders once the debt is converted into equity.

Equity Value

The equity value is the market value of the company's outstanding shares. Investors in convertible debt look at the equity value as a way to determine the company's future growth potential (and hence stock price increases), which can impact the conversion decision.

Event of Default

The event of default is a situation where the issuer of the convertible debt is in violation of the debt agreement. The event of default can result in the acceleration of the debt amounts due and payable, conversion of the debt into equity or dismissal of the rights and privileges of the holder.

Exchange Offer

An exchange offer is a proposal where the issuer offers to exchange outstanding convertible debt for new debt with better terms, such as a lower conversion price, longer maturity, or fewer restrictive covenants.

Exit Multiple

The exit multiple is the expected returns multiple at which the convertible debt holder will be paid back their investment once the company goes public or is acquired. This exit multiple determines the potential gain in value for the debt holder.

Face value

The face value of a convertible debt refers to the value the debt will have at maturity. This is the amount of money the issuer will owe to the investor when the debt reaches its maturity date.

Fiduciary duty

This refers to the legal responsibility of a person or entity to act in the best interest of another party. When a company issues convertible debt, they have a fiduciary duty to ensure that the interests of the debt holders are protected.

Fixed conversion price

A fixed conversion price is the price at which convertible debt can be converted into equity. This price is predetermined at the time of issuance and does not change.

Fixed income

Convertible debt investors receive a fixed income stream in the form of interest payments until the debt is converted into equity.

Floor price

A floor price is a minimum price at which the convertible debt can be converted into equity. This provides a safety net for investors and ensures that they receive a minimum return.

Forced conversion

A forced conversion occurs when the issuer of the convertible debt forces the conversion of the debt into equity, even if the investor does not wish to convert.

Full ratchet

A full ratchet is an anti-dilution provision that ensures that if the company issues new shares at a lower price than the convertible debt, the debt holder will receive additional shares to compensate for the dilution.

Funding round

A funding round refers to the process of raising capital for a business. Convertible debt is often used in early-stage funding rounds to provide short-term capital.

Future equity

Convertible debt is a hybrid security that has both debt and equity characteristics. The equity component comes into play when the debt is converted into equity at a later date.

Future financing

Convertible debt is often used by companies as a bridge to future financing rounds. The debt can provide short-term capital while the company prepares for a larger financing round.

Golden Handcuffs

Golden handcuffs refer to a provision in the convertible debt agreement that incentivizes bondholders to hold onto their bonds until maturity, rather than selling them on the secondary markets. This is achieved by offering a premium coupon rate or other incentives to the investors who hold onto the bonds until maturity.

Governance Clause

A governance clause is a provision in the convertible debt agreement that sets out the rights and obligations of the issuer and the bondholders. This clause typically includes provisions related to financial reporting, auditing, and decision-making processes. The governance clause is designed to protect the interests of both parties and avoid disputes over the terms of the agreement.

Grace Period

The grace period is a provision in convertible debt that allows the issuer to defer interest payments for a specified period without being deemed in default. This period is usually six months, and the interest that is calculated on the principal during the grace period is called deferred interest. The difference between the principal and the total amount outstanding is referred to as accrued interest.

Gray Market

The gray market refers to unofficial or unregulated trading in a security, such as convertible debt, before it is listed on a formal exchange. These trades take place between investors and are not subject to exchange rules or regulation.

Green Bonds

Green bonds are a type of convertible debt that is linked to environmentally-friendly projects. Proceeds from the sale of these bonds are typically used to finance sustainable infrastructure, clean energy, and other green projects.

Green Shoe Option

A greenshoe option, also known as an over-allotment option, is a provision in the underwriting agreement that allows underwriters to purchase additional shares of convertible debt from the issuer. This option can be exercised for a period of up to 30 days after the initial public offering, and is typically used to stabilize the stock price in the secondary market.

Greenium

Greenium is a term used to describe the premium that investors are willing to pay for green bonds. This premium is due to the perceived environmental and social benefits associated with the projects that are funded by these bonds.

Gross Proceeds

Gross proceeds refer to the total amount of funds that the issuer receives from the sale of convertible debt. This figure includes any upfront fees, underwriting discounts, and commissions paid to underwriters. Gross proceeds are calculated as the price of the convertible debt multiplied by the total number of shares to be issued.

Gross Spread

The gross spread is the difference between the price at which underwriters sell convertible debt to investors and the price at which they bought it from the issuer. This spread represents the underwriter's compensation for the risk and effort required to market and sell the convertible debt.

Guaranteed Convertible Bonds

Guaranteed convertible bonds are a type of convertible debt that are backed by collateral, such as assets or cash. This type of bond typically offers a lower yield than unsecured convertible bonds because the issuer has less risk.

Haircut

A haircut is a reduction in the market value of a security due to a perceived increase in risk. Convertible debt securities may be subject to haircuts during periods of market turmoil.

Hedge funds

These are investment vehicles that often invest in convertible debt securities as they offer attractive returns while reducing the overall risk of the portfolio.

Hedge ratio

The hedge ratio is the ratio of the notional amount of options held to the notional amount of convertible debt held. It is used to determine the number of options required to provide a hedge for the convertible bond held.

Hedging

Convertible debt holders may use hedging strategies to protect themselves from any downside risk including purchasing put options, shorting stock or selling short-dated futures.

Hidden dilution

The conversion of convertible debt to equity can lead to hidden dilution where the number of shares issued increases but there is no explicit increase in the outstanding shares.

High-yield bond

A high-yield bond is a speculative bond issued by a company that has a lower credit rating than investment-grade bonds. A convertible bond can also be a high-yield bond if the issuer has a lower credit rating.

Historical conversion premium

The historical conversion premium is the average difference between the market price of the company's stock at the time of issuance and the conversion price of the convertible debt security.

Holders

These are the individuals or entities that possess the convertible debt security and can exercise their right to convert it to equity in the company.

Holder's conversion option

This gives convertible debt holders the right to convert their debt into equity at a predetermined conversion ratio. The conversion may occur at any point during the life of the convertible bond, subject to any restrictions in place.

Hybrid security

A convertible debt security is a type of hybrid security that possesses both debt and equity characteristics.

Inflation Protection

Inflation protection is a feature of some convertible debt offerings that adjusts the conversion ratio to account for inflation, as measured by the consumer price index (CPI).

Insolvency

Insolvency is a situation where a company is unable to pay its debts to its creditors when they fall due. It is an important consideration for lenders, investors and shareholders when deciding to invest in the convertible debt of a company.

Interest Coverage Ratio

Interest coverage ratio is a financial metric used to assess a company's ability to service its debt obligations. It is calculated by dividing the company's EBIT (earnings before interest and taxes) by its interest expense, and is an important factor in determining the creditworthiness of a company issuing convertible debt.

Interest Rate

Interest rate is the amount of interest charged by the issuer of the convertible debt on the amount borrowed by the lender. It is usually expressed as a percentage of the principal amount and determines the amount of return expected on the investment.

In-the-money Conversion

In-the-money conversion is a situation where the convertible debt can be converted to common stock at a higher price than the current market price of the stock.

Investment Horizon

Investment horizon is the time period for which an investor plans to hold the convertible debt. It is an important factor in determining the investor's potential returns from the investment.

Investment Value

Investment value refers to the value of convertible debt as an investment, taking into account market conditions, interest rates, and other factors that affect the return on investment.

Investor Call Option

An investor call option is a feature included in some convertible debt offerings that allows the investor to convert the debt into equity before the maturity date of the debt.

Investor Rights

Investor rights are a set of legal rights granted to investors who purchase convertible debt, including the right to receive interest payments, convert the debt to equity, and participate in shareholder votes.

Issue Price

Issue price is the price at which the convertible debt is initially offered to investors. It is an important factor in determining the potential returns from investment in the convertible debt.

J curve effect

A term often used to describe the fact that initial returns of a startup investment may be negative before they turn positive in the medium-to-long-term. Convertible debt investments often go through this period, as it takes time for the startup to grow and establish itself in the market.

J-curve debt

A term used to describe the steep upward trajectory that convertible debt can experience when a company reaches a certain stage of maturity or gains momentum in a particular market. The J-curve effect is usually observed when the startup is on the verge of a major breakthrough, such as a new investment or product launch that could push its value upwards.

Joint and several liability

An obligation where two or more parties are equally responsible for the repayment of debt, with each party being on the hook for the full amount. Convertible debt may have joint and several liability clauses, meaning each investor is responsible for the entire amount of the convertible debt.

Jumbo CDs

Large certificates of deposit whose face value exceeds $100,000. Jumbo CDs can be used as collateral in certain convertible debt offerings, where the issuer pledges the CDs as security in the event the debt defaults.

Jumper

An investor who holds a convertible security and chooses to convert it into equity, either in part or in full. Jumpers tend to be sophisticated investors who are confident in the long-term potential of the company and believe that the equity offer a higher return in the long-term.

Jump-to-convert

A term used to describe the automatic conversion of convertible debt into equity as soon as a company reaches a predetermined trigger, such as a certain valuation or date. This can be more favorable to investors who want to take advantage of sudden growth in the company's potential value.

Junior debt

Debt that is subordinated to other debts in terms of priority in the event the borrower defaults. Convertible debt may also have a junior or subordinated claim in the capital structure compared to other forms of debt.

Junior Note

A type of debt that is subordinate to the senior debt, which means that if liquidation occurs, the junior noteholders are paid only after the senior noteholders. Convertible notes can be junior notes for equity investors past preferred shareholders but with similar downside protections to that of a senior investor.

Junk bond

High-yield bonds issued by companies with a lower credit rating grade. Convertible bonds can be classified as junk bonds if they are issued by companies that are deemed to have a higher potential risk of default. As such, their convertible debt securities may have higher interest rates to compensate investors for the higher risk.

Just-in-time (JIT) funding

A type of financing where the amount of funding needed to hit a specific milestone is delivered in increments aka "tranches" just as enough funding is required at specific time intervals to keep the business moving forward, instead of receiving one lump-sum investment all at once. Convertible debt is sometimes utilized in the form of JIT funding, as it allows investors to track the progress of their investment and make adjustments in real time.

Keeping investor confidence

Maintaining investor confidence is critical for any company looking to raise capital, whether through convertible debt or any other means. This involves being transparent and open about the company's financial performance and prospects, as well as communicating effectively with investors.

Key terms

These are terms that are critical to understanding convertible debt. They include things like the conversion price, conversion ratio, and maturity date. Understanding these key terms is essential to understanding how convertible debt works.

Kicker

This is a feature that can be added to a convertible debt offering to make it more attractive to investors. Essentially, it provides some extra incentive or reward for investors if the conversion terms end up being particularly favorable.

Kick-out rights

These are rights that investors may have to force the company to repurchase their debt at a premium or to convert it into equity early. These rights are typically granted to protect the investors and incentivize the company to perform well.

KISS

This stands for "Keep It Simple Security" and is a term used to describe a type of convertible debt offering that is designed to be simple, easy to understand, and investor-friendly.

KISS principle

The KISS (Keep It Simple, Stupid) principle is a design philosophy that emphasizes simplicity and avoids unnecessary complexity. In the context of convertible debt, it can be applied to the structure of the offering, the terms of the debt, and the communication with investors. By keeping things simple, companies can reduce confusion, reduce the risk of misunderstandings, and make the offering more attractive to investors.

Knockout provision

This is a provision that can be included in the terms of a convertible debt offering. It essentially stipulates that if the stock price falls below a certain level, the debt will be canceled or converted into something else.

Know your rights

As an investor in a convertible debt offering, it is important to understand your rights and obligations. This includes knowing when and how you can convert your debt into equity, what happens if the company goes bankrupt, and how you can exercise any other rights that you may have.

Know-how

This term refers to the knowledge and experience that is required to properly structure and execute a convertible debt offering. It involves understanding the various terms involved, the legal aspects of the offering, and other critical factors.

KPIs

Key Performance Indicators are metrics that companies use to track their performance and measure success. In the context of convertible debt, KPIs may be used to determine whether the company is on track to meet certain goals or targets, which could impact the conversion terms of the debt.

Lender of record

The financial institution or entity that is responsible for collecting principal and interest payments from the borrower.

Leverage ratio

A financial metric used to measure the amount of debt a company has relative to its assets or equity.

Lien

A legal claim on a borrower's property used as collateral for a loan.

Limited partner

A partner who contributes capital to a business but does not have control over its operations or management.

Liquidation preference

The preference given to convertible debt holders to receive payment before other types of creditors or shareholders in the event of the company's liquidation.

Loan covenants

Terms and conditions attached to a loan agreement that a borrower must meet in order to maintain the loan.

Loan maturity

The date on which the outstanding balance of a loan is due and payable.

Loan to value ratio

A financial ratio used by lenders to assess the risk of a loan by comparing the value of the loan to the value of the underlying collateral.

Lock-up period

A period during which shareholders or debt holders are restricted from selling their shares or debt securities.

Long-term debt

Debt that is due in more than one year from the date of issuance.

Market Capitalization

The market capitalization is the total value of a company's outstanding shares of stock. It's important to know the market capitalization of the company to determine the potential return on investment in case of a conversion.

Maturity Date

The maturity date is the date when the convertible note is due and payable. It's the date when the investor has the right to convert the debt into equity if the conversion event hasn't occurred.

Minimum Return

The minimum return is the amount of equity that the investor is guaranteed to receive at maturity if the conversion hasn't already happened. It acts as a protection against downside risk in case the company fails to meet certain conditions.

Multiple Conversion Features

Multiple conversion features are added to the convertible debt to provide more flexibility to the investor. It allows the investor to convert the convertible note into a different class of equity or at a different conversion price.

Negative covenants

These are restrictions placed on the issuer of the convertible debt, such as limits on borrowing, paying dividends or making acquisitions. These covenants are meant to protect the investors' interests.

New money conversion feature

This is a feature that allows a new investor to convert their investment into equity, while the old note holders who do not wish to convert maintain their position as note holders.

No discount convertible debt

This is a type of convertible debt that does not offer a discount on conversion, meaning that the investor would convert the debt into equity at the same price paid by new investors at the time of sale.

No maturity date

This is when the convertible debt has no set maturity date, meaning that the investor can hold the debt indefinitely until a conversion event occurs.

Non-cash interest

This refers to the interest payments made to the investors in the form of something other than cash, such as equity in the company or even more convertible debt.

Non-participating convertible debt

This refers to a form of convertible debt where the investors are not entitled to participate in any additional return beyond the principal and interest. In other words, they do not get any equity or ownership in the company.

Non-qualified financing

This refers to any financing round below a certain threshold amount. Convertible debt issued during non-qualified financing rounds is typically converted into equity at a discounted price.

Non-transferability

This refers to the restriction placed on the ability to sell or transfer the convertible debt to others.

Note

This refers to a written promise to pay a certain amount of money on a specific date. Convertible debt is often in the form of a note.

Notice of conversion

This is a formal notice given by the investor to the issuer stating their intention to convert the convertible debt into equity.

Offering memorandum

A written document that outlines the details of an offering of convertible debt, which is presented to investors. The offering memorandum usually includes information about the issuing company, financial information, use of proceeds, and potential risks.

Officer's certificate

A document signed by a representative of the issuing company stating that all of the information provided in the offering memorandum is true and accurate to the best of their knowledge. The officer's certificate is required as part of the closing documentation for the offering.

Operating agreement

An agreement that outlines the management and operation of a limited liability company (LLC). If the issuing company is an LLC, the operating agreement would be included in the offering memorandum and would specify the rights and responsibilities of the investor and the company.

Option pool

A specific number of shares of a company set aside for future issuance to employees or consultants. This pool is created as part of the company's convertible debt financing round. The idea behind an option pool is to create incentive for employees, aligning their incentives with the company's success.

Optional conversion

A provision in convertible debt that allows the holder of the security to choose whether or not to convert the debt into equity. In some cases, the conversion may be mandatory, but in other cases the holder may have the option to convert at a set price or to retain the debt until it matures.

Organizational costs

The costs incurred when a new company is formed. Organizational costs include legal fees, accounting fees, and other expenses related to setting up the company, and can be capitalized and amortized over time. When a company issues convertible debt, the organizational costs can be deducted from the proceeds of the offering.

Original issue discount

A discount that represents the difference between the face value of a convertible debt security and its original issue price when it is issued. This discount is essentially the interest that is paid upfront, rather than over time. The original issue discount can increase the effective interest rate of the security significantly.

Outstanding shares

The total number of shares of a company that have been issued and are currently owned by shareholders. When a company issues convertible debt, the outstanding shares will increase if the debt holders choose to convert their debt into equity. Knowing the number of outstanding shares is important for calculating a company's market capitalization and other important financial metrics.

Over-allotment option

Also known as a green shoe option, this is an option that allows the underwriter of a convertible debt offering to purchase additional shares from the issuing company if demand for the securities exceeds expectations. This option allows the underwriter to stabilize the price of the securities and reduce volatility.

Ownership dilution

A reduction in the percentage of ownership a shareholder has in a company, typically resulting from the issuance of new shares. When a company issues convertible debt, it often includes the right for the debt holders to convert their debt into equity at a set price, which can result in ownership dilution for existing shareholders.

Participation

Participation is a provision in a convertible debt agreement that allows investors to participate in the company's future equity financing rounds. This means that they have the option to convert their debt into equity at the same terms as the new investors in the financing round.

Pay-to-Play

Pay-to-play is a provision in a convertible debt agreement that requires investors to participate in future equity financing rounds in order to maintain their investment. If they do not participate, they may face penalties or have their debt converted into equity at a lower rate. This is meant to incentivize investors to continue supporting the company's growth.

Post-Money Valuation

The post-money valuation is the value of a company after it receives a new investment. It takes into account the money invested and the pre-money valuation. This value will determine the number of shares the convertible debt will convert into.

Premium

The premium is the additional amount of money that investors may be required to pay when converting their debt into equity. This amount is added to the principal amount and is typically a percentage of the conversion price.

Pre-Money Valuation

The pre-money valuation is the value of a company before it receives a new investment. It is important to know this value when issuing convertible debt, as it will determine the conversion price of the debt into equity. The pre-money valuation can be determined through different methods, including discounted cash flow analysis or market comparables.

Price Cap

A price cap is a provision in a convertible debt agreement that limits the conversion price of the debt into equity. This protects investors from the risk of the company being valued too high when they convert their debt into equity. It sets a maximum price at which the debt can be converted into equity.

Principal Amount

The principal amount is the total amount of money borrowed by the company through the issuance of convertible debt. This amount will determine the amount of equity the investor will receive upon conversion. The principal amount may also include interest or other fees associated with the debt.

Put Option

A put option is a provision in a convertible debt agreement that allows the investor to sell back their debt to the company at a predetermined price. This protects investors from the risk of the company not performing as expected and offers them an exit strategy.

Qualified Financing

A qualified financing is a financial round where a company raises a specific amount of capital from accredited investors. In convertible debt, the qualified financing triggers a conversion event, which allows the investor to convert their debt into equity at a pre-determined valuation cap. The qualified financing serves as a measure of progress for the company and provides a clear path for debt conversion.

Qualified Institutional Buyer (QIB)

A Qualified Institutional Buyer is an institution that meets SEC requirements for investing in securities. In convertible debt, the presence of a QIB indicates that the investment is from an institution that is knowledgeable, experienced, and able to invest large amounts of capital. Having a QIB as an investor is seen as a positive signal to other investors and can help trigger the qualified financing round needed for the conversion.

Quality of Investor

Quality of investor refers to the level of experience and reputation of the investor putting money into a company. In convertible debt, a reputable investor can give the company credibility and attract other investors, thus increasing the chances of success. High-quality investors are also more likely to convert their debt into equity, giving the startup necessary capital to grow.

Quantified Discount

A quantified discount is a percentage or dollar amount subtracted from the conversion price of convertible debt when the debt is converted into equity. The discount compensates the investor for the risk of investing in a startup and the fact that the equity price may be considerably higher than the current price at the time of conversion.

Quantity of Debt

Quantity of debt refers to the total amount of convertible debt an investor provides to a startup. The quantity of debt has a direct impact on the conversion terms; the more debt an investor provides, the more favorable their conversion terms.

Quarterly Reports

Quarterly reports are reports issued to shareholders that give an update on a company's financial performance every three months. In convertible debt, investors use quarterly reports to track the startup's performance against projections, financial position, and growth prospects. The reports are essential in providing investors with insights into whether the debt-to-equity conversion is likely and the potential risks involved.

Quasi-Equity

Quasi-equity is a hybrid financing method that combines features from both equity and debt financing instruments. In convertible debt, the quasi-equity aspect arises from the option to convert the debt into equity. It provides the investor with the security of receiving their capital back in the event of a default while still giving them the potential for equity returns.

Questions to Ask

Questions to ask refer to the due diligence process investors go through before funding a startup. In convertible debt, investors must ask various questions to determine if the debt-to-equity conversion is fair and beneficial to all parties. The questions to ask include the startup's metrics, financials, and growth projections.

Quick Assets

Quick assets are assets that can be easily converted into cash within a short period. In convertible debt, quick assets are relevant during the valuation of the conversion price. Quick assets provide investors with an assurance that even in the event of a default, the investment can be liquidated within a short time to compensate for the debt.

Quiet Period

The quiet period refers to a period when a company is prohibited from making announcements about their financial performance or material events. In convertible debt, the quiet period often happens when a startup is going through a significant financing round, and the details have not been publicly announced. The quiet period helps in reducing the chance of insiders making unfair gains from the information asymmetry.

Ratchet Clause

A Ratchet Clause may be included in convertible debt agreements, providing for an adjustment to the conversion price in certain circumstances. For instance, in a down-round financing, the conversion price may be reset based on the lower valuation of the issuer's stock, effectively diluting the original investors.

Redemption Right

Redemption Right means that the issuer has the right to redeem the convertible debt from the investor, usually at a specific time or upon the occurrence of a particular event. The investor's right to convert the debt into equity would be negated if the issuer chooses to exercise the Redemption Right. The redemption price is typically the par value of the debt or the outstanding principal amount plus any accrued interest or premium.

Registration Rights

Registration Rights provide the holder of convertible debt with the right to require the issuer to register the underlying shares for public trading. This enables the investor to sell the shares more easily once they are converted. The registration process may entail additional costs and expenses, and the issuer may be reluctant to grant registration rights to all debt holders.

Repayment Schedule

The Repayment Schedule outlines the timeline for repayment of the convertible debt. The schedule typically includes the principal, interest rate, and repayment frequency, among others. Sometimes, the schedule may be structured such that the interest payments are rolled up, and the principal is payable only upon maturity or conversion.

Reset Date

The Reset Date is the date on which the Reset Price of the convertible debt is adjusted, pursuant to contractual provisions or periodic adjustment mechanisms. The Reset Date may coincide with the issuer's earnings announcement, for example, or the exercise of certain shareholder rights.

Reset Price

The Reset Price refers to the price at which the convertible debt would convert into equity. It is established when the debt is issued and may reflect the current market price of the issuer's stock or a premium over it. The Reset Price may change over time based on contractual provisions or periodic adjustment mechanisms.

Restrictive Covenants

Restrictive Covenants are contractual provisions that bind the issuer, investor, or both parties to certain restrictions or obligations. They aim to protect the interests of the parties and ensure compliance with agreed terms. Common examples of Restrictive Covenants include restrictions on additional debt, limitations on asset sales, or dividend distributions.

Rights Offering

A Rights Offering is a financing mechanism that allows existing shareholders to buy additional shares of the issuer's stock at a discounted price. The convertible debt may have a provision that entitles the holder to participate in a Rights Offering, either by converting the debt into equity or receiving an option to purchase additional shares at a specified price.

Secured Debt

A form of convertible debt that is backed by collateral, such as assets or property, that can be seized in the event of a default on the loan.

Security Conversion Ratio

The ratio that determines how many shares of common stock a convertible security can be exchanged for upon conversion. This ratio can vary depending on the terms of the convertible debt.

Seniority

A term that describes a convertible debt that has priority over other forms of debt or equity in terms of repayment in the event of liquidation or bankruptcy of the company.

Shareholder Approval

The process by which a company's shareholders must approve the terms of a convertible debt offering before it can be issued. This provides a level of oversight and protection for investors.

Startup Valuation Cap

The maximum valuation at which convertible debt can be converted into equity during a future financing round. This helps protect early investors from being diluted in the event the company's valuation has significantly increased.

Stated Maturity Date

The date on which the principal and any unpaid interest on convertible debt becomes due and payable.

Stock Options

An agreement that gives an investor the option to purchase shares of common stock in the company at a specific price during a certain period. These options can be used to convert convertible debt into equity at a later date.

Strike Period

The length of time during which a convertible security can be converted into shares of common stock. This period typically lasts a few years and can be extended in certain circumstances.

Strike Price

The predetermined price at which a convertible security can be exchanged for shares of common stock upon conversion. This price is typically set at a premium to the current market price of the stock.

Subordination

A term that describes convertible debt that is subordinate to other forms of debt or equity in terms of repayment in the event of liquidation or bankruptcy of the company.

Term

Term Sheet

Underlying Asset

This refers to the asset that will be used to pay back the debt in the event of default. For convertible debt, the underlying asset can be converted into equity at the discretion of the investor. This provides a degree of flexibility in the repayment terms.

Underlying Price

The underlying price is the value of the underlying asset that will be used to determine the conversion price of the convertible debt. The conversion price is typically set at a premium to the underlying price, to provide investors with additional upside potential.

Underlying Shares

This refers to the shares of common stock that the convertible debt can be converted into. The number of underlying shares is determined by the conversion ratio specified in the offering documents.

Underwriter

An underwriter is a financial institution that acts as an intermediary between the issuer of the convertible debt and potential investors. The underwriter helps to market the debt to investors and can provide expertise in structuring the offering.

Unfunded Commitment

An unfunded commitment is a promise by an investor to provide funding in the future, usually in the form of a loan or equity investment. Convertible debt can include unfunded commitments, which allow companies to raise additional capital in the future without having to sell more equity.

Unitranche Financing

This is a type of financing that combines senior and mezzanine debt into a single loan. The loan is typically structured as a single lien security and is often used in leveraged buyouts or other acquisitions where a large amount of debt is needed.

Unsecured Convertible Note

This is a type of convertible debt that is not secured by collateral. Unsecured convertible notes are typically only used by companies with strong credit ratings and are often issued in smaller amounts than secured convertible debt.

Unsecured Debt

Unsecured convertible debt is not backed by collateral. This type of debt is riskier for investors, as there is no underlying asset that can be liquidated to satisfy the debt in the event of default.

Upside

The upside refers to the potential for appreciation in the value of the equity shares that the convertible debt can be converted into. Investors are attracted to convertible debt because of the potential for upside, even if the underlying company does not perform well.

Use of Proceeds

This refers to how the funds raised through the issuance of convertible debt will be used. The use of proceeds must be disclosed to investors in the offering documents.

Valuation Cap

The maximum pre-money valuation of a company that investors will use to determine the conversion price of their convertible note. If the company's valuation exceeds the cap, the conversion price will be based on the cap rather than the actual valuation, which protects the investor's equity stake.

Valuation Discount

A discount investors receive when converting their convertible debt into equity shares. This is used to account for the additional risk investors take on with convertible debt, as these securities are considered riskier investments than straight equity.

Valuation Event

A significant corporate event, such as an IPO or acquisition, that triggers the automatic conversion of convertible debt into equity shares. Valuation events are typically used to protect investors, as they ensure that investors are not "left holding the bag" if the company fails to reach a certain valuation threshold.

Variable Interest Rate

A type of interest rate structure in which the interest rate charged on a convertible note fluctuates with a benchmark interest rate or market index. This structure can be used to protect investors from risk, as rising interest rates will lead to a higher rate of return on investment.

Venture Capital

Financing provided to early-stage, high-growth companies by investors who are seeking long-term returns through equity or convertible debt investments. Companies that receive venture capital funding are typically considered high-risk, high-reward investments.

Venture Debt

Debt financing provided to startups and early-stage companies with high-growth potential. Unlike traditional debt financing, venture debt is typically structured as convertible debt, which allows lenders to benefit from future equity appreciation.

Venture-backed IPO

An initial public offering (IPO) that is financed by venture capital investors. Venture-backed IPOs are often seen as a mark of success for startups, as they allow early investors to monetize their investments and provide a source of liquidity for the company.

Vesting

The process by which employees or other stakeholders receive full ownership of stock or stock options over a period of time, often tied to certain milestones or performance metrics. Vesting is important for startup employees who may receive stock options as part of their compensation package.

Volatility

The degree of variation in a company's stock price over time. High volatility increases the risk of investors who hold convertible debt, as the likelihood of a poor return on investment increases if the stock price falls.

Voting Rights

The rights provided to convertible debt investors to vote on certain company matters, such as the election of board members and major corporate actions. Typically, convertible debt investors will have the same voting rights as common shareholders.

WACC

The weighted average cost of capital (WACC) is a financial metric that calculates the cost of a company's capital by weighting the cost of debt and equity. Convertible debt is a hybrid of debt and equity, and as such, can be included in the calculation of WACC.

Wall Street

Refers to the financial district of New York City where numerous large financial institutions and banks are located. Convertible debt is often traded on Wall Street through investment banks and other financial institutions.

Wallflower

A term used to describe a type of convertible debt that is unpopular with investors and is not being actively traded or bought. A wallflower convertible debt may be difficult to sell or convert to equity.

Warrants

These are a type of security that gives the holder the right, but not the obligation, to buy a specific number of shares of the company at a specific price. Warrants usually have a longer expiration date than other securities and are often used as an added incentive for investors to purchase convertible debt.

Window

Refers to a particular time period in which a company's convertible debt can be converted to equity. The window is usually specified in the terms of the loan and can vary depending on the specific agreement.

Wipeout

A term used in the event of a company's bankruptcy or liquidation. If the company doesn't have enough assets to pay back its creditors, some or all of the convertible debt may be wiped out, leaving the investors with nothing.

Withstand

Refers to the ability of a company to weather financial storms and remain financially stable. Convertible debt can help a company withstand economic downturns by providing additional funding without requiring collateral.

Working Capital

This refers to the capital that a company has available for daily operations. Convertible debt can be used to increase a company's working capital, allowing them to invest in inventory, equipment, and other expenses.

Worthy

A characteristic of a company that is attractive to investors. Convertible debt can be a sign of a company's worthiness, as it shows that investors are willing to bet on its future success.

Writing

This refers to the process of creating the convertible debt agreement, which includes the terms of the loan, conversion ratio, maturity date, and other specifics. The writing stage is crucial in order to ensure that all parties are in agreement with the terms of the agreement.

Yield Curve

Yield curve, represents the relationship between the bond yields and bond maturities. Yield curves help to provide an overview of what the market expects will happen to bond yields as they approach maturity. Understandable and observable patterns of yield curves may help investors to make a more clear decision about the right time to invest in bond markets.

Yield Enhancement

Yield enhancement is a strategy that is often used in fixed-income securities to increase the yield when a portfolio is expected to be flat or stable over a short period. Yield enhancement can be achieved with the use of structured securities like convertible bonds.

Yield on Convertible Debt

Yield on convertible debt, also known as YOC, is an estimate of convertible debt's total return that factors in the yield to maturity and the conversion value if it is converted into a certain number of shares of common stock. The YOC measure enables the investors to check whether it is better to invest in convertible debt or the common stock. If the YOC is higher than the stock's dividend yield, convertible bonds become more appealing to investors.

Yield to Maturity

Yield to maturity, also known as YTM, is the total return anticipated from a bond or other fixed-income security if the security is held until its maturity date. When convertible debt's conversion feature is utilized, the yield to maturity calculation changes, and it is typically the lower of the bond's yield to maturity and the return on the stock.

Yield-to-Average Life

Yield-to-average life, or YTAL, is a measure of the total return of a bond if it is held until the average total time remaining until the bonds call or maturity date. The average life of call dates can be calculated by determining the length of time until the first mandatory selection date or the date on which the bond is most likely to be redeemed.

Yield-to-Conversion

Yield-to-conversion, or YTC, represents the yield on convertible securities that offers an attractive total return if the bonds subsequently convert into common stock. YTC is the yield attained on the convertible bond if assigned to the common stock as soon as possible but has a standard time constraint (such as ten days after the notice of redemption).

Yield-to-Customers

Yield-to-customers, or YTCu, is a measure of the yield on a bond security that is computed based on the actual cash flows received by the investor. YTCu takes transaction fees and other costs into account to get a more realistic picture of the bond's real yield.

Yield-to-Price Ratio

Yield-to-price ratio is the measure of the effective income a bond can offer given its current price in the market. The yield-to-price ratio can help investors to compare the expected yield of a bond to other investment opportunities available in the market.

Yield-to-Worst

Yield-to-worst, or YTW, is defined as the yield of a bond or other fixed-income security if it is not held until maturity. It refers to the lowest yield an investor may expect from a bond structure in a worst-case scenario. In case the bond is redeemed early, the fixed rate bond becomes essentially a call option on the stock, hence, the yield-to-worst is the lower of the Yield-to-Call and the Yield-to-Maturity.

Yield-to-Worst Call

Yield-to-worst call, or YTWc, is a measure of the worst-case yield for the bondholder in the case of an early call. When a bond is callable, the issuer will redeem it early, and the least yield available during a premature redemption is the yield-to-worst call.